*"Funny, thrilling and wise…the best sort of theatrical biography: the sort that thoroughly entertains."*
*--David DeWitt, The New York Times*

# JAMES BALDWIN

## *A SOUL ON FIRE*

a short play by

# HOWARD B. SIMON

*Edited by Charles Reese*

*Foreword by David Leeming*

*Afterword by Forrest McClendon*

# WHAT PEOPLE ARE SAYING ABOUT JAMES BALDWIN: A SOUL ON FIRE!

*"The best sort of theatrical biography; the sort that thoroughly entertains. With humor, style and raw emotion, A Soul on Fire embraces its chosen territory with enthusiasm. All stage biographies should be served so well."*
**--David DeWitt, New York Times**

*"Playwright Howard Simon conjures up a dilemma that neatly captures the conflict Baldwin faced between his art and his activism."*
**--Charles McNulty, The Village Voice**

*"Howard Simon's performance play, James Baldwin: A Soul on Fire is an engrossing poetic display of the religious, political, and internal turmoil that marked the life of one of the great writers of the 20th century".--***Jeanette Toomer, Back Stage**

*"There are only two actors in this story, but you feel the stage is filled with many more.."--***Lisa Giordano, Show Business News**

Glover Lane Press
A Division of Azaan Kamau Media
4570 Van Nuys Blvd Suite 573
Sherman Oaks, CA 91403

ISBN-13:978-0615583273 (Glover Lane Press)

ISBN-10:061558327X

Book Cover, Book Design, and Publishing By Azaan Kamau of
Glover Lane Press
Archival Soul on Fire Logo by Sean O'Halloran
Charles Reese Biography Photo by Jose E. Montano

For a list of titles by Glover Lane Press Please contact Azaan Kamau of Glover Lane Press at gloverlanepress@gmail.com or http://gloverlanepress.webs.com

The Mission of Glover Lane Press is to Uplift, Empower, Elevate the Masses by providing American Jobs. Every book published by Glover Lane Press and it's many imprints, is printed and manufactured in the United States of America, ensuring and maintaining American employment.

# CONTENTS

# HISTORICAL HIGHLIGHTS

This short performance play started out as a gift from one brother to another brother; followed by an initial reading with friends, a standing room only workshop presentation, a critically acclaimed Off-Broadway production in New York City, along with a series of hybrid staged readings and archival screenings in museums, art galleries, theatre festivals and poetry/coffee houses from 1999 -2011. Each step has always re-ignited a new interest in the amazing life of this play prior to and after the untimely death of our playwright, Howard B. Simon.

The official publishing of this play in 2012 marks the 25th anniversary of the writer/civil rights activist, James Baldwin's physical departure from the literary, art and culture scene in 1987 at his home in St. Paul de Vence, France. The following section briefly highlights a few of those historical moments about "the short play that keeps pressing onward and upward."

JAMES BALDWIN: A SOUL ON FIRE was first performed as a reading project guided by the playwright Howard Simon at the John Houseman Theatre, 450 W. 42nd Streets, New York, NY in Studio #B on February 6, 1999. The cast was as follows:

| | |
|---|---|
| JAMES BALDWIN | Charles Reese |
| ETHEREAL | Forrest McClendon |
| Stage Directions | Ron Jones |

JAMES BALDWIN: A SOUL ON FIRE received its first workshop production as part of The Eclectic Exorcism New Works Theatre Festival, curated by Jeffrey Miller.

Presented by The Sage Theatre @ Raw Space at 529 West 42nd Street, New York, NY on June 13, 14,19, 20, 1999.

Directed by Chuck Patterson; Costumes by Fredi Walker-Brown; Lighting by Jack Brown; Video & Sound by Sean O'Halloran; Stage Manager: Laura Johnston. The cast in order of appearance was as follows:

| ETHEREAL | Forrest McClendon |
| JAMES BALDWIN | Charles Reese |

JAMES BALDWIN: A SOUL ON FIRE received its Off-Broadway opening on April 9, 2000 in New York City. The Henry Street Settlement/Recital Hall Theatre at 265 Henry Street, New York, NY. Presented by The New Federal Theatre, Woodie King, Jr., Producing Director.

Directed by Chuck Patterson; Production Stage Manager: Jacqui Casto; Sets/Technical Director:Terry Chandler; Lighting Design: Antoinette Tynes; Costumes: Anita D. Ellis; Video & Sound Design: Sean O'Halloran; Property Mistress: Laura Johnston; Dramaturge: Matt Korahais.

The cast in order of appearance, was as follows:

| ETHEREAL | Forrest McClendon |
| JAMES BALDWIN | Charles Reese |

# ACKNOWLEDGEMENTS

The family of Howard Simon: Tracy, Antoinette & Patricia Simon; Dr. Tracy Durrah-Broadnax; Tony Kushner (Howard Simon's mentor at NYU); Richard Wesley (NYU); David Leeming (Baldwin's Biographer); Harry Belafonte ; Forrest McClendon: Myla Churchill Barrett; Sheryl Ellison Ponds; Sean O'Halloran; Spencer Scott Barros; Lee Dobson; Matt Korahais; Chuck Patterson;Woodie King, Jr and The New Federal Theatre ( with kudos to the late Wayne Grice); Elaine Charnov; Teddy Yoshikami; Myles Gordon; American Museum of Natural History(New York); George Alexander; Marcia Pendelton;Irene Wiley; Dwayne Barnes; Chris Grosset; Fredi Walker Brown; Laura Johnston; Jacqui Casto; Anita Ellis; Antoinette Tynes; Pat White; Kwame Braithwaite; Richard Termine; The 275 Adelphi Crew (pre-gentrification in Fort Greene); Brenda Brunson Bey; Spring McClendon; Selma Jackson & 4W Circle of Art & Enterprise; Jen Brissett & Indigo Café & Books; Maurine Knighton; Special thanks and appreciation to CCH Pounder (Pounder Kone Gallery LA); the late Ben Bradley (Fountain Theatre); the gracious Doris Roberts; Paula Mitchell Manning and Jose Luis Valenzuela at the New Los Angeles Theatre Center (LATC) for the support of the performance readings in 2007 in Los Angeles, CA. My late mother: Mrs. Mary Alice Reese; My late sisters: Shirley Reese and Otherie Reese-Wright; My sisters: Minnie Reese & Wanda Reese; My brother, Roy Reese; Gilbert Wright III ; Jessica Wright;"Q" Street & The Shaw Community (Washington, DC);Ellis Gratts(for years of kindness and generosity); Darryl Gallien; Armelia McQueen; Azaan Kamau & Glover Lane Press; Jeffrey King & In the Meantime Men's Group; Robert Holmes; Patricia Belcher; Patricia Dawson; Michael Ajakwe; Penny Ludtke; Jose E. Montano; Rosalyn Myles; Joyce Guy; Julie Hebert; Tommy Brewer; Claudine Brown; Elliot Johnson (Eagles Nest@

Hollywood Hills); Bill Cosby; Malcolm Jamal Warner & Pam Warner; Lamar Alford (my amazing grace mentor) and Morehouse College; Ron Jones; Virginia Capers; The Brooklyn Arts Council; Jean Michel Albert (Marseille Web Festival)

Samuel Legitimus & Collectif James Baldwin (The French Translation); Atoy Wilson; Brice Tripard (Paris Host); Abdel LaBlack, Hafed & Hakeem (Arles Host); Patricia Haillot (Aix en Provence Guide); Hassan Barrett; William Mathis; Danny Frazier; Keith Chaplain; Wanda Lee Evans; Kenny Long; Desmona Dallas Harris; Leslye Joy Allen;Leticia Tish James; Curtis Young;Rita Kuoh;Grazell Howard;Clarence R. Williams; Cece Antoinette; Barbara Roberts;Donald Farber Esq;Ann Farber; Willete Klausner; Michelle Crenshaw; Ruth Body; Deborah Mickens-Lynex and the Mickens Family Tree;Cleo King;Camille Thornton; Clark Peters; Lisa Davis,Esq; Sendroff & Associates; BW Grant Barnes, Esq; Thomas Brown; and Kelly Mills-Williams.

A Very Special Thanks and Appreciation:

Chuck Patterson: our first director for your time, energy and passion in guiding us from the workshop to the Off-Broadway Production.

Woodie King Jr: our first producer for the lunches at the Time Café with Howard Simon and myself. For saying "Yes" to the project.

Forrest McClendon: for being my brother and friend for over 20 years. You really make me look good on stage. Thanks for staying with me through all the journeys and adventures. Kudos to you for now being a Tony Award Nominee 2011 for your wonderful work in the Broadway production of The Scottsboro Boys. Looking forward to the Baldwin project revival nationally and internationally.

Howard B. Simon: Thank you my brother and friend for the gift that keeps on giving. Thanks for being an ancestor that continues to guide and watch over this little play.

For anyone that I may have forgotten, simply charge it to my head and not my heart. I remain grateful. And so it is.

# FOREWORD

Writing in the New York Times on April 12, 2000, David Dewitt called the off Broadway production of Howard B. Simon's James Baldwin: A Soul on Fire "the best sort of theatrical biography" and praised the "passionate performance" of the lead actor, Charles Reese. Howard Simon has passed away, but Charles Reese is still with us, and he has made it his life's work to keep the public's attention on the play and on the late James Baldwin's soul

as revealed in the play. The publication of this book during the year marking the 25th anniversary of Baldwin's death is one result of Mr. Reese's commitment.

I met Charles Reese 10 years ago at Indigo Books & Café in Brooklyn. He informed me that evening that Howard Simon had been inspired to write his play by the chapter in my Baldwin biography that dealt with a little known but central event in Baldwin's life. In May of 1963, three months before the March on Washington, Baldwin had written to then Attorney General Robert Kennedy deploring the failure of his brother's administration to treat civil rights as a moral rather than a political issue. The Attorney General agreed to meet in New York with Baldwin and a group of influential blacks—a group that would include, among others, Lena Horne, Lorraine Hansberry, Harry Belafonte, Kenneth Clark and a freedom Rider, Jerome Smith—to discuss the "Negro" issue. The meeting would be a disaster, but that is another story. What Simon focuses on in his play is what he imagines to have been Baldwin's inner state before he left his apartment for the meeting on May 24th.

As a Baldwin friend and biographer I can attest to the accuracy of Simon's imagination and, as one who has seen the play, to Reese's interpretation of Simon's vision. Baldwin was in many ways a "burning soul." A man who loved the simple joys of life—eating, singing, loving. But he was above all a prophet, a man possessed by a driving and demanding need to remind his people—black and white—of how they had lost sight of the right path. He and his friends would remind Kennedy of that moral blindness. When in the meeting Kennedy suggested that blacks, like his fellow Irishmen could pull themselves up by their bootstraps and that in 40 years or so one might even become president, Baldwin reminded him that blacks had arrived here long before the Irish, and that an Irishman was now a president whereas blacks were "still required to supplicate and beg you for justice." James Baldwin was, of course, right, and, ironically, Kennedy was close to right in his rhetorical estimate of the time it would take for a black man to become president.

David Leeming
James Baldwin's Biographer, Friend and Former Secretary
New York, NY
September 13, 2011

# THE ANCESTORS SPEAK

*Human freedom is a complex, difficult and private thing. If we can liken life, for a moment, like a furnace, then freedom is the fire which burns away illusion. Any honest examination of the national life proves how far we are from the standard of human freedom with which we began." (Nobody Knows My Name)*

*James Baldwin, Writer/Civil Rights Activist*
*August 2, 1924 – December 1, 1987*

*"Today is the beginning of ending colonized notions of self proclaiming liberty where our poems are our songs...holding us up; walking together in the spirit shouting: Hallelujah....we are moved, we are changed!" (Today Feels Like A Poem)*

*Howard B. Simon, Writer/Activist*
*October 26, 1962 – April 12, 2000*

# THE CHARACTERS

JAMES BALDWIN, *American writer born in Harlem, NY, Expatriate (Paris, France) and Civil Rights Activist. His books: "Go Tell It On The Mountain" and "Giovanni's Room" made him an international icon. His book, "The Fire Next Time" published in 1963 caught the attention of the Attorney General Robert Kennedy of the United States.*

ETHEREAL, *Spirit-like figure who embodies all of the following roles:*

Lorraine Hansberry, *Playwright, first African American woman to have a play, "A Raisin in the Sun" produced on Broadway in 1959.*

Harry Belafonte, *Entertainer, singer, actor and civil rights activists who worked closely with Dr. Martin Luther King Jr.*

Lena Horne, *Singer, actress, first African American to receive a major contract with a studio in Hollywood. Starred in the film, "Stormy Weather" for which she sang the title song.*

Jerome Smith, *Young African American Freedom Rider.*

Henry Morganthau, *Jewish Producer/ WGBH-TV.*

Peter, *a fictional character inspired by James Baldwin's book, "Tell Me How Long The Train's Been Gone"— Black Christopher Chapter . Peter was created for the purpose of the dramatic structure of this play by Howard Simon. Peter represents "everyman" who is simply trying to survive.*

**Editor's Note**: *This play is a re-imagined experience inspired by an historical event: The Baldwin/Kennedy Meeting. However, the late writer, Howard Simon uses creative and other theatrical conventions as a tool to explore Baldwin's innermost passions and the tone of what was happening in 1963, one of the most catalytic years in the struggle for the civil rights movement for Blacks in the United States.*

# THE PLAY

THE TIME: MAY 24, 1963

THE PLACE: New York City.

An apartment in the West Village.

THE SET: A small apartment with simple décor. A bed, night stand, TV, phones - (including a phone that has buttons to push that puts one caller on hold). Other parts of the set are "suggested" - ie: the shower, French windows that open to the terrace.

*The lights fade on Laverne Baker's recording of "Soul on Fire."*

*The lights slowly rise, We hear sounds of thunder as JAMES BALDWIN enters in a silk bath robe, eyes closed, as if floating in a dream – he is being pushed, pulled, and led by ETHEREAL, a spirit like figure.*

*As they cross the stage to the bed, Ethereal sings the traditional song "Keep Your Eyes On The Prize." Then they ceremoniously get into the bed.*

*ETHEREAL (Sings)*

*Oh Brother, I know the road is long, but you gotta'
hold on, don't give up on your dreams.*

*And, Oh Sister, keep your eyes on the prize, gotta'
hold on, don't give up your dreams. You see…*

*Paul and Silas bound for jail, had no money for to
make their bail,*

*Keep your eyes on the Prize, Hold on.*

*Paul and Silas thought they were lost, dungeon shook
and the chains come off,*

*Keep your eyes on the Prize, Hold on.*

*Hold on… Hold on. Keep your Eyes on the prize,
Keep your eyes on the prize,  keep your eyes on the
prize… hold on.*

*(The song ends--the lights are up, but dimly lit)*

*JAMES BALDWIN  is asleep in the plush bed with
ETHEREAL in a white flowing cape with his body
wrapped around JAMES' body. Their limbs entwined.
They are one.*

*Ethereal rises up, from a still sleeping James, and
hovers above him in the bed waving an olive branch.
He bends down, kisses James gently on the lips, and
touches his eyelids.*

*Ethereal slithers off the bed, floats through the room, his white cape billowing about, and sings the traditional hymn, "Wade in the Water." He touches items - the telephone, the TV, as if he is "blessing them," "Christening them" to come alive.*

*Suddenly, as if enacting an invocation to conjure up a storm, Ethereal rushes around the room striking jarring poses. First, a bolt of light shines through him like lightning. Second, thunder crashes as Ethereal "becomes" a set of French doors standing above the head of James Baldwin - the doors open, thunder, lightning, rain.*

*James Baldwin tosses and turns in the throes of a nightmare, then violently bolts up in a sitting position.*

## JAMES

Ahhhh!… Those got damn doors again. I'm tired of this shit! All this damn money I'm paying to live here… my shit better work. Peter…Peter… Peter… boy, I know you ain't gone nowhere.

*(James gets out of bed, slips into a long, elegant, silk robe.)*

## JAMES

After all the shit I gave you… and you're not going to be in my bed when I wake up?… These damn doors.

I got to get somebody in here to fix this shit. This don't make no kind of sense... I can't believe it. The sky was so clear last night. There was no prediction for rain... Oh my God, what time is it? Oh, damn - no electricity. Damn, I have a meeting with the Attorney General of the United States, and I'm late.

*(James picks up a glass and Ethereal fills it with red wine, James gulps it down.)*

Shit, all of America is late as far as I'm concerned. Me and my entourage will be there Mr. Attorney General. You'll just have to wait for us.

Where is my wrist watch? Let me light a candle so I can half see myself think.

*(Without skipping a beat Ethereal hands him a candle & lights it)*

*(The lights rise)*

*(Ethereal presents him with a watch and a letter)*

### JAMES

Oh, my watch and a letter from Peter... Whew, my Lord, his name suits him - Peter. What is it about a fine black cat? I just couldn't help myself last night. I mean, there I was, all alone at a bar on 125th Street. What is a man to do? Along comes Peter. Peter, Peter, Peter, Peter Pumpkin eater had a wife and couldn't keep her. Put her in a pumpkin shell and then he came to my house last night. It's 6:30 AM. Our meeting is at noon. I guess I need to get my costume ready for this afternoon's drama. Well, at least the boy is literate.

*(James reads the letter. Ethereal curls around him like a protective blanket.)*

Shit, spoke too soon... D-E-E-R ...Jay... I just hate it when they get the name wrong. My name is James... James Arthur Baldwin... Muthafuckers can't get your name right, but they want shit from you...

JAMES/ETHEREAL (as Peter)

*(reads together)*

"Had a good time. See you round. Oh, I needed some dough to get back uptown with. Hope  you don't mind the loan..."

JAMES

Yeah, how much this muthafucka take me for... Shit, can't see a damn thing... Got damn, he took all my money. Got damn... But Peter sure was fine. All those bitches in that bar wanted him... they were all huddled together. Don't  no man want a man that acts like a woman... and then you have the frustrated broke down old Negro Literati of the Renaissance, uptown... sitting in another corner all frustrated in

16

straight lace… I hear when y'all talk about me.

*(Ethereal comes up behind him, James leans the back of his head on Ethereal's chest, runs his hands up and down his arms behind him)*

And you went to church last Sunday hearing the gibberish of your hell fire preachers and you lusting after that incredible, make your knee drop, Black man and I got him… I got him… so talk if you want to… maybe you talk too much…Let me blow this damn candle out before I set my damn house on fire.

*(James lights a cigarette off the candle, he and Ethereal blow out the candle together)*

### JAMES

Let me think… Yes, I have a meeting with the Attorney General of the United States. Now, there's a man! He was so manly at his home in Virginia, Hickory Hill… Yeah, he's on a hill alright. I don't think he has a clue as to what is ripping the nation apart by the threads, but he's a family man with his children, who will never ride the filthy subways in their lives. They vacation at Hyannis, and they just can't see why the Negro can't work himself up to that level. Why, there are a few of you that are good. Hell, look at you… Yeah, look at me. Hell yeah, look at me with your condescending, controlling, and condemning eyes… look at black me.

*(James disrobes. He turns upstage and faces Ethereal who has now "become a shower" as he drapes his robe around James, one hand overlapping the other in continuous movement throughout the following, we hear water running.)*

I got to wash my body. Lord knows I don't want to go nowhere stinking. It is a sin and an abomination against God. I got to wash the ash off my skin...

My black ugly skin. My daddy always said I was ugly... then everyone said it. "Oh Black Jimmy Baldwin is Ugly"... Ugly by whose standards? What's ugly is Black inequality if you want to speak on U-G-L-Y, Ugly is when I'm in the White House, not as a hired help, but came through the front door... Some official white man without a title asks someone behind me "Who is the ugly Black man?"... And I'm in the White House just like him... Ugly is when world renown Black entertainers like Paul Robeson and Josephine Baker receive better public accommodations abroad than in their own country... Perhaps it's not the Black man's country... I got to wash the ash off my knees... But it's not the white man's either. The native said the land belonged to the great one... I got to wash the ash off my knees... Ugly is when you can't see me from your pulpit reverend up in Harlem because I got sugar in my shoes... I got to wash the ash off my knees... always on my knees for one reason or another... sometimes these folks make me want to wash off all my skin and be born anew lifted up as in a host or multitude of giving  praises… shouting in the morning time… Calling on my Lord Jesus Christ, Hallelujah.

*(James flings the shower curtain aside and strikes a pose in the image of A CROSS. Ethereal dresses him in a robe – like a Christening gown)*

### JAMES

For he has anointed me to be he that can stand persecution for persecution sake… bringing down upon those who do not love me the wrath of my father.

*(As if he's evoking a moment from Baldwin's  "Amen Corner" James sings "My Soul Will Be A Witness For My Lord," Ethereal joins in the jubilee behind him.)*

### JAMES

Oh Lord what manner of man is this – all nations in him are blessed. All things are done by his hand. *(Sings) He spoke to the sea and the sea stood still, now ain't that a witness for my lord – ain't that a witness for my lord. My soul will be a witness for my Lord.*

*(James gets the audience involved in the song, clapping along, singing along, call and response. At the end of the song, James collects himself as though*

*he's a character in Baldwin's "Go Tell It On The Mountain" or Martin Luther King Jr. giving a sermon)*

## JAMES

What shall I wear to meet the Attorney General? Of course there will be others, but what must I wear? I have called on others to be by my side standing hand and hand with a new attitude for the final is near. It is now or dooms day…which will it be Mr. Attorney General… family man, of Hickory Hill, and Hyannis… Descendant of those railroad workers who were always over worked with unfair pay. What shall I wear to see you? Shall it be of gold bronze and ruby red sun from which I flowed through Mother Africa…What I wear and how I wear my hair have become confusing apparatuses of control… Administered by the un-informed wearing uniforms of oppressive colors. What shall I wear to meet the man having no name? Shall I wear raging blue where millions of my ancestors drowned wading through the passage…Where Tituba flew across… Oh, shall I wear the ocean blue… Blue is what I am cause *(sings the blues)* "that man done left me"… Peter, Peter, ah shit, what's the use. Let me put my song on… to soothe my soul.

*(Ethereal, "as Lena Horne" sashays up behind him, sings in his ear)*

ETHEREAL (ala Lena Horne)

*(sings)*

*Don't know  why, there's no sun up in the sky, stormy weather, since me and my man ain't been together, seems like it's rainin' all the time…*

JAMES

For now I'll wear white.

I know I have to put something on my stomach this morning. I need my energy today. I'm taking a meeting with Mr. Attorney General Kennedy. I wonder what he's eating for breakfast. I think I'll have me some grits. Yeah, grits stick to your ribs. Master ate grits. They were cheap and could feed plenty of slaves.  Gave them energy to pick that cotton from sun up to sun down. Oh shit now… I got to keep this fire low. Lord knows I don't want nobody's lumpy grits. I can't stand it. My Momma said …

ETHEREAL (JAMES' MOMMA)

"If you can't cook grits then you trifling."

JAMES

Now, I heard we got to stay away from that pork. They said it's killing us.

## ETHEREAL (JAMES' MOMMA)

The bible say don't eat it…

## JAMES

I'm going to look that up, but I'm going to fry me some slab bacon while I do it. Now I know master ain't give us no bacon or no other parts of the hog. He gave us the Chitlins… the intestines. The place where shit comes out of the hog. We took them and used them. We were nourished by them. And Lord, shit is what's going to fly today with Mr. Kennedy. We're tired Lord… You hear that Lord? We're tired of these white folks, you hear… Cause we're about to take action one way or another. It's time for a change. "What does the Negro want?" he asked. What in the hell do we want? The same as you mutherfucka… Lord knows I need my energy for these white folks here today.

*(Like a Pentecostal, "fire and brimstone" preacher, James rushes around the stage, sings "I Been Running For Jesus A Long Time, I'm Not Tired Yet" as Ethereal joins him, playing a tambourine)*

*(Ethereal, from another area of the space, picks up A PHONE. *An alternative action could be Ethereal picking up phones placed around the set.)*

*(James' phone rings)*

JAMES

Damn, just as I was about to get down… *(picks up phone)* Hello…

ETHEREAL (PETER)

Hello baby…

JAMES

Peter, Peter… it's good to hear you. Why did you leave?

ETHEREAL (PETER)

I don't know, but I had a good time last night.

JAMES

Well, why did you leave?

ETHEREAL (PETER)

Look man, my old lady need some money to feed the kids.

JAMES

Whose kids?

## ETHEREAL (PETER)

One or two of them mine… Hell, but they all ain't mine.

*(Ethereal picks up another phone – IT RINGS)*

## JAMES

Why don't you give her the money you got from my wallet this morning?

*(His other line rings again)*

## JAMES

Peter hold on please… *(he clicks the phone to switch to the other line)* Hello.

## ETHEREAL (HENRY MORGENTHAU)

Hello, Mr. Baldwin, I'm Henry Morgenthau the third, not the second, that was my dad and he was a son of a bitch.

## JAMES

Morgenthau of WGBH TV? Could you hold please? My other line is ringing. Hello… Peter?

ETHEREAL (PETER)

Yeah, I had to take care of some important business.

JAMES

What?

ETHEREAL (PETER)

That's why I don't have any money to give my lady.

JAMES

You're going to have to call me back.

ETHEREAL (PETER)

Why?

JAMES

Because I have an important call on the other line that I must take.

ETHEREAL (PETER)

Like what I'm talking about ain't?

JAMES

You don't understand.

ETHEREAL (PETER)

No, you don't understand that I ain't hangin' up 'til I get an answer from you.

JAMES

Well fine... go ahead... hello...

ETHEREAL (HENRY MORGENTHAU)

Yes, Mr. Baldwin I saw you on the cover of May seventeenth's issue of Time Magazine. Impressive!

JAMES

Well thank you kindly sir... How may I assist you?

ETHEREAL (HENRY MORGENTHAU)

I hear that you are having a meeting with the Attorney General today.

JAMES

One hears many things... I hear the students across the country's south land sitting-in and demanding equal justice... I hear the faint sound of freedom songs as city police and state troopers gas and beat peaceful marchers... How have you heard?

ETHEREAL (HENRY MORGENTHAU)

I have heard through freedom. Please appear on my show after your meeting with the Attorney General and tell my audience about it.

JAMES

I invite you to attend the meeting and hear it for yourself. Meet at my agent's office Bob Mills. Twelve noon sharp. Bye.

ETHEREAL (HENRY MORGENTHAU)

Wait, what's your agent's address?

JAMES

Let freedom direct you… hello…

ETHEREAL (PETER)

Yeah, man I just need a small loan.

JAMES

Loan what?

ETHEREAL (PETER)

Money, cash, dough, loot, you got plenty. You up 'round all those crackers, you should have plenty money.

JAMES

I don't like the way this is sounding.


ETHEREAL (PETER)

You don't like. Do you think I really like being up in the bed with you?

JAMES

Well why did you do it?

ETHEREAL (PETER)

Sin… sin has got me… it's got you… sin… can you spare some money for my lady? *(Ethereal dials another phone)*

JAMES

Oh, there is my other line. I got to go…


ETHEREAL (PETER)

No, let me hold on…

JAMES

Bye… Hello…

## ETHEREAL (LORRAINE HANSBERY)

Hello Jimmy…

## JAMES

Good morning Lorraine…

## ETHEREAL (LORRAINE)

Don't good morning nothing'. We need a plan for today…

## JAMES

Don't worry I got it under control.

## ETHEREAL (LORRAINE)

What is it… because I'm tired of hearing about the bible and non-violence. The real revolution is coming and Negroes aren't going to be afraid to die under police fire.

## JAMES

OK, you're fired up for this meeting.

## ETHEREAL (LORRAINE)

Yes I am.

JAMES

You're not drunk are you?


ETHEREAL (LORRAINE)

Drunk with the ripe wine of revolution. I'm sick and I'm tired.

*(Ethereal dials another phone)*

JAMES

Hold on Lorraine... hello...

ETHEREAL (PETER)

Don't hang up on me. You weren't too busy for me last night.

JAMES

Listen, I have a very important meeting with an important government official...

ETHEREAL (PETER)

Does this government official know that you like men? Do they know that you're a Homosexual?

JAMES

I have no idea... hold on...

## ETHEREAL (PETER)

I don't feel like playin' no games here.

## JAMES

I'm not playing anything. You called me... Oh boy, hello, Lorraine.

## ETHEREAL (LORRAINE)

What is the problem?

## JAMES

I have a male friend of mine who wants to play games while I have important work to do.

## ETHEREAL (LORRAINE)

Get rid of him...

## JAMES

It's not an easy task.

## ETHEREAL (LORRAINE)

James, we have to think, strategize, map out... You have to stop thinking with your foreskin, Jimmy.

JAMES

But he is drop dead gorgeous.

ETHEREAL (LORRAINE)

Yeah, and now you can get rid of him.

JAMES

Yeah, the Black man just needs a little help.

ETHEREAL (LORRAINE)

Amen to that, but right now we need a real plan for Mr. Kennedy.

JAMES

Lorraine, we're going to meet the man.

ETHEREAL (LORRAINE)

I think I'll write something.

JAMES

Another play?

ETHEREAL (LORRAINE)

Naw, not this time. This time I'll write instructions for a real revolution.

JAMES

You just can't write revolution. Revolution is action...

ETHEREAL (LORRAINE)

Didn't the founding white men of this country map out revolution back in 1776?

JAMES

No, they were framers of oppression. Real revolution comes from the people...

*(Ethereal dials another phone)*

ETHEREAL (LORRAINE)

Yeah, power to the people...

JAMES

Hold on... hello...

ETHEREAL (HARRY BELAFONTE)

Jimmy, it's Harry....

JAMES

Mr. Belafonte...

## ETHEREAL (HARRY)

Harry, call me Harry…

## JAMES

Ok Harry, I have Lorraine Hansberry on the other line…

## ETHEREAL (HARRY)

Ah Lorraine, tell her I said Walter Lee in "A Raisin In The Sun" should've been my part.

## JAMES

I sure will. What can I do for you this morning?

## ETHEREAL (HARRY)

I have an idea for a plan of action for today's meeting.

## JAMES

Lorraine and I are discussing that very matter… hold on…hello Lorraine, guess who's on the other line?

## ETHEREAL (PETER)

I don't give a damn, and this ain't no bitch.

JAMES

Peter, I don't have time for this foolishness. We had a
nice night together. Good bye.


ETHEREAL (PETER)

Don't you hang up on me nigga…

JAMES

Hello, Lorraine…

ETHEREAL (HARRY)

No, it's Harry…

JAMES

Oh shit, I'm getting all mixed up.

ETHEREAL (HARRY)

Don't you worry because we're all in this mess
together. We'll get you through it.

JAMES

Thank you!

## ETHEREAL (HARRY)

We must let the Attorney General know that we are searching for the moral healing of America...

## JAMES

Let me run that by Lorraine... Lorraine?

## ETHEREAL (LORRAINE)

Yeah, was that another boyfriend?

## JAMES

Baby, no... it's Harry Belafonte...

## ETHEREAL (LORRAINE)

Oh how nice, Mr. Belafonte...

## JAMES

Harry, call him Harry...

## ETHEREAL (LORRAINE)

*(Sings) I'm just wild about Harry and Harry's wild about me.*

## JAMES

He's in a solemn mood. He's talking about the moral healing of America...

## ETHEREAL (LORRAINE)

Well, I have nothing against that, but the time to act is now because brothers and sisters are getting tired and pretty soon it will be By Any Means Necessary.

## JAMES

Lorraine, I'm trying to get through all that girl, but the man is gorgeous.

## ETHEREAL (LORRAINE)

Who?

## JAMES

Harry, umm umm, he's a fine Black man. And you know I saw "Carmen Jones" six times just to see his chest!

*(Ethereal dials the phone)*

## ETHEREAL (LORRAINE)

Oh Lord.

## JAMES

There is another call. If it's that boy...

ETHEREAL (LORRAINE)

You won't do a thing but listen. Don't forget we got business this morning, Negro...

JAMES

Hello Peter, don't call here no mo'...

ETHEREAL (LENA HORNE)

Who's Peter?...it's Lena Horne.

JAMES

Lena, chile, I was just listening to you this morning because my man done walked off and left me and it seems as if it is storming all around me.

ETHEREAL (LENA)

Well darling, you better raise up an umbrella and get ready for our meeting with the Attorney General. I'm just checking in... making sure everything is all right because I'm Lena and special that way. Anything I can do for you?

JAMES

Nothing I can think of...

ETHEREAL (LENA)

This meeting should take place uptown, but I'm glad

it's downtown because I ain't going up there talking about civil rights. Let Mr. Attorney General take the government's policies on civil rights to Harlem. I don't want to get shot.

JAMES

Yes Lena there is one thing only you can help me with…

ETHEREAL (LENA)

Yes?

JAMES

What color are you wearing?

ETHEREAL (LENA)

Black, it's a serious color.

JAMES

I'll see you this afternoon.

ETHEREAL (LENA)

Love.

JAMES

Hello… Harry?

ETHEREAL (HARRY)

Yes, Jimmy you seem to be a busy man.

JAMES

I was running your idea of moral healing to Lorraine, and she says it's good, but we must stress action. What actions must we take to represent this moral healing?

ETHEREAL (HARRY)

How about a march?

JAMES

It must be something that all Americans can see, recognize and join in. We need Dr. King's help...

ETHEREAL (HARRY)

He's very sorry that he can't make the meeting, but...

JAMES

But he's nervous around me?

ETHEREAL (HARRY)

Don't be ridiculous. Dr. King is in high profile and he just has to carefully schedule his meetings and appearances. He still is a minister of a church.

JAMES

Oh, I understand.  I understand more than you know.
He must carefully take meetings.

ETHEREAL (HARRY)

He has asked Dr. Kenneth Clark to represent him.

JAMES

Dr. Clark, great, we may now have a fighting chance.

ETHEREAL (HARRY)

Counsel from the wise is most wise.

JAMES

I must tell Lorraine… hold please, Lorraine, the man
is sending goose pimples all over my back.

ETHEREAL (LORRAINE)

I know what action we can take…

JAMES

Harry says a march.

ETHEREAL (LORRAINE)

No, we need something more powerful than a march
for moral healing…

## JAMES

I need Harry…

## ETHEREAL (LORRAINE)

We need to ask the Attorney General to ask the President to escort a Black child in Mississippi to an integrated school…

*(Ethereal dials another phone)*

## JAMES

Hold on… hello…

## ETHEREAL (PETER)

You think you can just hang up on me? Well, now you have made me mad.

## JAMES

Look man…

## ETHEREAL (PETER)

Yeah, man look… look for that new book you're working on… the one you showed me last night… Where is it?

## JAMES

Man please don't play with my work.

## ETHEREAL (PETER)

Don't play with me.

## JAMES

I can't find my manuscript. Do you have it?

## ETHEREAL (PETER)

I might and I might not.

## JAMES

Why are you doing this to me?

## ETHEREAL (PETER)

I'm not doing anything. I just need some money for my old lady.

## JAMES

Wait a minute, I have to clear the other lines.

## ETHEREAL (PETER)

You do that. Meanwhile, I'll get back with you.
*(hangs up)*

## JAMES

Lorraine?

ETHEREAL (HARRY)

No, Harry… listen, it's getting late and if we're to be prompt, we better get moving.

JAMES

Well, I think we should ask the Attorney General to get the President to escort a Mississippi black child to school while the nation looks on.

ETHEREAL (HARRY)

What good will that do?

JAMES

It represents a deep moral commitment. A point would be made with the President's presence. If any dares spit on that child, they would also spit on the President and the nation.

ETHEREAL (HARRY)

Point well taken. It's a go as far as I'm concerned. I have to go. See you later today.

*(Ethereal dials another phone)*

JAMES

Lorraine, you ain't going to believe this shit…

ETHEREAL (LORRAINE)

Harry didn't like my idea.

JAMES

Oh no, he loved it… Peter…

ETHEREAL (LORRAINE)

Not him again…

JAMES

Yes, and this one has stolen my manuscript that I'm supposed to hand to my publisher today.

ETHEREAL (LORRAINE)

Niggas and flys…

JAMES

None of that talk…

ETHEREAL (LORRAINE)

What are you going to do?

JAMES

I'm waiting for the man to call me.

ETHEREAL (LORRAINE)

Now you're waiting on his call... Ain't this about nothing.


JAMES

Hold on, there's the other line, it must be him...

ETHEREAL (LORRAINE)

Well I have to do something with this hair before I meet anybody's Attorney General...

JAMES

Hold on for one minute... Hello, Peter...

ETHEREAL (JEROME SMITH)

Hello, may I speak with Mr. James Baldwin.

JAMES

Speaking... who's calling?

ETHEREAL (JEROME)

My name is Jerome Smith, and Miss Hansberry gave me your number and told me to contact you.

JAMES

Could you hold on for a moment, my other line is ringing.

ETHEREAL (JEROME)

Sure…

JAMES

Lorraine, who is this Jerome?

ETHEREAL (LORRAINE)

Oh, I nearly forgot. He is a young man who along with other people tried to integrate bus terminals and stations across the south. He was severely beaten by sheriffs in Mississippi. His presence and story are what we need today.

*(Ethereal dials another phone)*

JAMES

I have to get the other line. It's probably Peter.

ETHEREAL (LORRAINE)

Talk with Jerome… You'll find his story interesting… Got to run. Speak with you later.

JAMES

Hello…

ETHEREAL (PETER)

Yeah, have you given me any thought?

JAMES

Yes, I've been thinking - why are you doing this to me?

ETHEREAL (PETER)

Let's call it the Black man's burden.

JAMES

Do you plan to return my manuscript?

ETHEREAL (PETER)

Sooner or later, which ever comes first. I need some money.

JAMES

Can you hold on while I get this young man off the phone.

ETHEREAL (PETER)

So, you took up with another man already. You kind of work quick… I want one thousand dollars.

JAMES

I don't have that kind of money laying around the
house.

ETHEREAL (PETER)

You better find it or you won't find your book.

JAMES

Can you hold on?

ETHEREAL (PETER)

No, let me give you some time to think about it.
(hangs up)

JAMES

Hello…

ETHEREAL (JEROME)

Yes, Mister Baldwin… I don't want to take up much
of your time. I just thought since you were speaking
with the Attorney General, a very important man in
this country, that you would tell him that Black men
like me are tired of second class citizenship. My
grandfather fought in World War I and my dad fought
in World War II, and they both served their country
well only to return to racism, discrimination, and
segregation. We're mad and we're no longer going to

defend a country that doesn't defend all of her citizens. America is living a lie.

## JAMES

I think you need to join our meeting today and tell the Attorney General yourself, but know that you now will represent.

## ETHEREAL (JEROME)

And that I will… I will represent those who have faced segregation with fire hoses turned on them, dogs biting them, policemen beating them with clubs, and men and women lynched on lonely roads as their spirit cross the middle passage heading for freedom land… Yes, I will represent.

## JAMES

Come to the meeting with Miss Hansberry. She shall be your guide. Goodbye…

*(The phone rings repeatedly, James takes his time answering it)*

## JAMES

Hello…

## ETHEREAL (PETER)

Yeah, you have the money?

## JAMES

Maybe.

## ETHEREAL (PETER)

Don't play no games. You got the money?

## JAMES

How do I know you really have my manuscript?

## ETHEREAL (PETER)

Look Nigga, you know it ain't in your house.

## JAMES

It may not be worth that much to me.

## ETHEREAL (PETER)

That's not what I heard you tell that white man on the phone last night.

*(Throughout the following two monologues the dialogue overlaps with JAMES BALDWIN and ETHEREAL(PETER). There is an organic flow to the delivery.)*

JAMES (Overlaps with Ethereal/Peter)

I can't believe this Negro done stole my script. He can't do anything with it. They're my words. He can't use them the way I do, but he does recognize their value or else he wouldn't have stolen it. Maybe I can remember it or reproduce it, but writing is in the present. It is within a moment that a writer chooses a word and places it within a sentence which then gives the word life. To re-find, re-trace to re-place words. It might be easier to pay the man. After all, he's just running a hustle, and I did invite the man into my house.  And maybe the man will come back and touch me like he did before.

ETHEREAL/PETER (Overlaps with JAMES)

You told him how you just finished it. You were sending the only copy of the script to him. Then you told me… You showed me the entire script. Like I'm gonna read that shit you write…

ETHEREAL(PETER)

You do a lot of things when you're drunk. And I'm gonna add on an extra five hundred for thinking I was stupid. I want fifteen hundred dollars by twelve noon.

JAMES

That's impossible I have a very important meeting…

ETHEREAL (PETER)

With the Attorney General. Yeah, yeah, yeah… you told me all about that. Too bad, cause I want to see you at twelve noon.

JAMES

My brother will be here to give you the money, and you can leave the manuscript with him.

ETHEREAL (PETER)

No, no, no. When I do business I never go through third parties. I'll only deal with you. If you want your precious manuscript that will save the world from the great white man, be there at twelve noon.

*(Ethereal sings a line of "Stormy Weather" to taunt James. They both hang up the phones.)*

*( As James gets dressed he sings "Ain't Gonna Let Nobody Turn Me Around." Ethereal assists him in putting on a black suit and tie. James carries an olive branch in his left hand.)*

*(The intercom for the door buzzes)*

ETHEREAL (DOORMAN)

Mr. Baldwin, it's the doorman, your car is here.

JAMES

Thank you…

*(James keeps singing. The phone rings continuously)*

Hello…

ETHEREAL (LORRAINE)

Jimmy, it's Lorraine… our meeting with the
Attorney General is in twenty minutes. Why are you
still there?

JAMES

I'm waiting on my manuscript.

ETHEREAL (LORRAINE)

Your manuscript? What foolishness are you
speaking?

JAMES

Peter has the only copy of my new manuscript and I
need it back.

ETHEREAL (LORRAINE)

Can't you get it later… Our meeting…. You have to
be here. You're the leader.

JAMES

Who made me the leader? I never wanted to be in charge of anything.

ETHEREAL (LORRAINE)

Sometimes the yoke just falls on our shoulders and we must be strong to do what has been asked...

JAMES

But my book...

ETHEREAL (LORRAINE)

You'll write other books.

JAMES

The publisher is waiting...

ETHEREAL (LORRAINE)

Right now history calls you. Leave now.

*(James continues to sing "Ain't Gonna Let Nobody Turn Me Around" as he walks to the door and Exits.)*

*(Ethereal, alone for the first time, turns on the radio. We hear bits of songs from the sixties as he turns the radio dial. Ethereal does various sixties dances. A*

*moment passes--- Ethereal turns on the television –*
*we see different sound bites/visual  images of*
*pinnacle events from the Civil Rights Movement of*
*1963 ie: President Kennedy speaking on civil rights,*
*White Police men standing with their feet on the neck*
*of a black woman, Martin Luther King Jr. reading his*
*letter from the Birmingham jail, James Baldwin on*
*the cover of TIME Magazine.)*

*(Then, we see a close up image of James Baldwin on*
*the TV.  Ethereal joins the audience and watches the*
*WGBH TV program,  that Henry Morgenthau*
*referred to earlier, which features the actual footage*
*of James Baldwin being interviewed by Dr. Kenneth*
*Clark. They discuss the aftermath of the*
*Kennedy/Baldwin meeting.)*

*(James re-enters the apartment, the television*
*continues to play with the "real Baldwin" on the*
*screen.)*

## JAMES

The war is on Muthafucka  and something's going to
burn something's going to burn down… Wickedness
and fire, the devil is loose for we wrestle not against
flesh and blood but powers and principalities and
spiritual wickedness in high places. I know I didn't
leave this television on… trying to run up my bill…
you trying to run a whole lot of damn things…That
Robert Kennedy, the Attorney General is talking

shit... Meaningless Moral Gesture.... He calls "our plan" to get his brother, President John Kennedy to escort a Black child to school in the segregated south a meaningless moral gesture... He talking shit... how the Kennedy's as descendants of immigrants could point to a background of oppression. His family pulled themselves up. With luck, a Black man could be president in forty years. Forty years...Negroes were here long before the ancestors of the Kennedy's and the fact that a Kennedy is already the damn president (and the Attorney General) while the black man is still required to supplicate and beg YOU for justice is a meaningless moral gesture. Now I know I didn't leave the television playing... Um um, Peter, is that you? Are you here?

## JAMES

Where are you, cause I didn't leave the television playing... did I? I know I ain't crazy... drunk, maybe... high on reefer, none of your business, but I did not leave this set running...

*(James turns the television off)* But you better believe this country is running out... it is running out of time... running out of sync... running out of cash... where the man can spit on you and call you nigger and I best like it, if I want to live...

*(Ethereal dials a phone. James listens to the ringing phone before answering.)*

JAMES

Hello…

ETHEREAL (LORRAINE)

I rejoiced when I heard them say let us go to the
house of the Lord… But our house is burning down
brother. What shall we do?

JAMES

Sister Lorraine, Behold, the Lord will come with fire,
and with his chariots like a whirlwind, to render his
anger with fury, and his rebuke with flames of fire.

ETHEREAL (LORRAINE)

That history will remember these times with words
and photos of White men standing on the necks of
Black women.

JAMES

For by fire, and by his sword will the Lord plead with
all flesh: and the slain of the Lord shall be many.

ETHEREAL (LORRAINE)

I hope Mr. Attorney General realizes that real
resistance is coming. Maybe the meeting will lead to
some type of action. We were not a group of good
Negroes begging the white power structure to be nice

to Negroes. We are Black citizens saying that this is an emergency for our country, as Americans.

JAMES

God sent Noah the rainbow sign…no more water, the fire next time.

ETHEREAL(LORRAINE) /JAMES

*(sings) My Lord he calls me, he calls me by the thunder… the trumpet sounds within my soul – I ain't got long to stay here…*

JAMES

Stay strong sister…

*(The intercom for the door buzzes)*

ETHEREAL (DOORMAN)

Mr. Baldwin, it's the doorman, a boy left this package for you. Shall I bring it up?

JAMES

Please, thank you.

*(The doorbell sounds. James answers the door. He returns with a big envelope with a letter attached to it)*

## JAMES/ETHEREAL (PETER)

*(Reading the letter)*

"Your punk ass wasn't here…"

## ETHEREAL (PETER)

*(Continues reading the letter)*

"Don't you know this is no time to fool with a nigga. All that other meeting and shit is bull shit. I'm talkin' 'bout real livin' day to day on the real streets and you didn't help me, so fuck you. See you going to all these top meetings with white folk and you haven't considered what I need. I need some money for my old lady. You write about her and me in your stories; so why can't you give us some money. We just tryin' to live. Now see if you can live without your book. Here are the ashes. Maybe you can spread that shit around the world for peace and brotherhood."

(Ethereal exits)

*(The phone rings.. James picks up the phone and then hangs up. James slowly opens up the package – visibly horrified at its contents – the sight of his book, burnt to ashes, represented by a ceremonial cloth)*

JAMES

You burned my book, boy. A nigger that can't read
worth a damn burned my book. But this is what I get
when I mess with fucked up trash like you,
muthafucka…And so now you feel good, don't you.
You feel real good knowing you've destroyed
something and someone… this makes you happy.

*(The phone rings louder)*

JAMES

The book that I wrote to help liberate muthafuckas
like you and you went and burned it…Everyman's
work shall be made manifest: for the day shall declare
it, because it shall be revealed by fire; and the fire
shall try every man's work of what sort it is.

*(James begins to ceremoniously DANCE with the
cloth of ashes. The phone rings louder.)*

JAMES

If any man's work abide which he hath built
thereupon, he shall receive a reward.

*(The phone continues to ring loudly as James listens
for a few seconds)*

## JAMES

If any man's work shall be burned, he shall suffer loss: but he himself shall be saved; yet so as by fire.

*(James rips the phone apart.)*

Just to be done with it. Not worry… not feel the agony of segregation… Not to be constantly looked at and examined as a specimen.

*(James makes a noose with the ceremonial cloth of his book ashes along with the phone)*

To be lifted up and taken somewhere where I can be alone… Somewhere I can rest… real rest. Not that get up and stretch your arms rest, but a change of mind.

*(James steps into the shower area, he puts the noose of the ceremonial cloth/phone around his neck and secures it for a hanging.)*

## JAMES

Christ hath redeemed us from the curse of the law: for it is written, cursed is everyone that hangeth on a tree.

*(Just as he hangs himself and begins to sway as if hanging from a tree, there is a knock at the door. Ethereal enters, rushes over to James Baldwin and saves him from the hanging facing upstage. Ethereal puts on a black beret, does a military about face, and faces the audience as a Black Panther.)*

## ETHEREAL (BLACK PANTHER)

The Honorable Minister of Defense Huey Newton of The Black Panthers Party requests your presence in the revolution of all Black People of the world... Power to The People!

*(Ethereal does a "Black Panther Salute" gesture and holds it)*

## JAMES

*(sings)*

Amen... Amen... Amen, Amen, Amen...

*(James joins him in the "Black Panther Salute" gesture, holds it.)*

*(The lights begin to slowly fade)*

## JAMES

*(continues to sing)*

Amen... Amen...Amen!

*(Thunder Sounds) (BLACK OUT)*

## END OF THE PLAY

# AFTERWORD

### A Gift: Howard B. Simon and Suzan-Lori Parks

Charles Reese called me at home in Philadelphia in early 1999. He needed somebody "right now" because he had "organized a reading of a new play" and his "roommate Spencer Barros isn't available." I said, "Yes, Charles, of course I will do it." Reese had been after his longtime friend Howard Simon to write him a one-man show about James Baldwin. To Charles' utter amazement, Howard presented him with the play as a birthday gift, but there was one catch: it called for a second actor in a new kind of multi-layered character.

In his new play, JAMES BALDWIN: A SOUL ON FIRE, Simon wanted to examine Baldwin's dual role as an artist and activist and he chose to do so at a critical moment in our nation's history. Simon probed Baldwin's inner psyche on the day of an important meeting—a real-life 1963 roundtable discussion on race relations between then-Attorney General Robert Kennedy and a group of prominent civil rights figures lead by Baldwin. The group included Lorraine Hansberry, Harry Belafonte, and Lena Horne among others. In addition to Reese as Baldwin, Simon wanted all of those "witnesses" for his story—ALL of them—and they would be played by what he called "a force of nature" named Ethereal. I was simply stunned by the challenge of the shape-shifting Ethereal—this Baldwin alter ego who portrays seven distinct characters across generation, racial, gender and class lines; in other words our world as Simon imagined that James might see it.

Luckily, I had been working "outside the box" with the incomparable Suzan-Lori Parks at the Wilma Theater in Philadelphia, who serendipitously mentioned that James Baldwin told her "to write plays." In THE AMERICA PLAY, Parks also re-imagines a chapter from our nation's history where the actor must play a multi-layered character. Simon, however, took this idea to a dizzying chameleonic level in one particular scene where he had James interact with Ethereal as ALL of these other figures.

That intimate reading of JAMES BALDWIN: A SOUL ON FIRE, for a group of fifty, took place at the John Houseman Theatre on 42nd Street and it changed the focus of my work as an artist and educator. Not only was I suddenly armed with new tools for building characters, but I also understood the power of theatre as a means for inspiring dialogue about important issues and why Howard saw the piece as not just a play but "a theatrical event." I was truly fortunate to be a part of the SOUL ON FIRE journey from its workshop at Sage Theatre Company's Eclectic Exorcism New Works Theatre Festival at Raw Space on 42nd Street to its Off-Broadway premiere at Woodie King's New Federal Theatre with noted actor Chuck Patterson as director and our good friend Matt Korahais as assistant director and dramaturge.

Sadly for us, Howard went home before he could read the favorable reviews of his play. Then, it was Reese who was "a force of nature" sending Howard home and pushing towards opening SOUL ON FIRE and performing it through two extensions. Charles Reese continues to act as a vigilant steward of the legacy of these two great writers of the 20th century, Howard Byron Simon and James Arthur Baldwin.
This play is Simon's gift to the inimitable Charles Reese (and ALL of us).

With my thanks, for years of friendship, kindness, support and guidance.

Forrest McClendon
Original Cast Member (Ethereal) & 2011 Tony Award Nominee, The Scottsboro Boy
November 11, 2011
Lancaster, PA

# AFTERWORD

## A Revival/Renaissance : 26 Years Ago...26 Years Later !

Twenty-six years ago... I journeyed to Paris, France with my
friend and colleague, the late playwright/poet, Howard B. Simon
(after our graduation from Morehouse College in 1985). We
were searching for James Baldwin. I had previously met Mr.
Baldwin in a brief encounter on the Morehouse campus back in
1981 while he was preparing for his book about the Atlanta
Child Murders (The Evidence Of Things Not Seen). Much to our
chagrin, James Baldwin was not in France in the summer of
1985 as we were told upon our arrival to his home in
the southern  part of France in St. Paul de Vence.  James
Baldwin was in the United States!

Twenty-six years later... I journeyed to Marseille, France (about
2 hours away from Baldwin's home) via an invitation from
producer, Jean Michel Albert to attend the first ever Marseille
Web Fest. My micro comedy web series, "WHO..." created by
Emmy Award winner, Michael Ajakwe was an official selection
from the USA.

And now twenty-six years later on October 26, 2011 (the late
playwright, Howard Simon's birthday), I am sitting in a small
café on the right bank in Paris, France sipping some coffee while
archiving my newest journey of my amazing destination to
James Baldwin—the ancestor, the writer, the civil rights activist,
the poet and prophet—only this time, I am bearing witness to
Baldwin's fiery spirit via a short play written for me by my
college mate, Howard B. Simon. Simon's performance play re-
imagines the lesser known Baldwin/Kennedy secret meeting of
1963 in New York City. This critically acclaimed Off-Broadway
play has now been re-engineered to a book version as a literary
tool to celebrate and re-ignite Baldwin's "burning soul," twenty
five years after his death in St. Paul de Vence on December 1,
1987.

"Burning soul" is how my friend and colleague, David Leeming (Baldwin's Biographer) described Baldwin's innermost passions in his thought provoking and heartfelt foreword.

Nineteen sixty-three (the time period of the Baldwin/Kennedy Meeting) marked the "burning soul" of the Civil Rights struggle in the USA. Nineteen sixty-three is considered to be the pinnacle year of the most catalytic events of the movement—beginning with the 100th anniversary of the Emancipation Proclamation to excerpts of Baldwin's The Fire Next Time (January 1963); Martin Luther King Jr's Letter From The Birmingham Jail (April 1963); Baldwin/Kennedy Meeting in New York City (May 1963); The brutal murder of Civil Right activist, Medgar Evers (June 1963); The March on Washington (August 1963); The Bombing of the Four Little Girls at the Sixteenth Street Baptist Church in Montgomery, Alabama (September 1963); and the assassination of President John Kennedy (November 1963). This was definitely a time of "FIRE" for change, and Baldwin along with many others paved the way with their fiery spirits through the power of the pen and the spoken word.

And here I am back in Paris, France 26 years later and Barack Obama, a black man of African descent is now the President of the United States of America. ( a forty plus year old prophesy that has now been full filled, based on a statement Kennedy uttered to Baldwin in the secret meeting of 1963 that serves as the premise to this re-imagined play by Mr. Simon). As a cultural architect for public engagement, I imagine that the celestrial spirits of James Baldwin and Howard B. Simon along with Bayard Rustin, Lorraine Hansberry, Countee Cullen, Zora Neal Hurston, Wallace Thurman, Bruce Nugent, Marlon Riggs, Essex Hemphill and so many other past artists/activists, continue to watch over and guide this new face of change in the United States and beyond.

It is my wish that this play book will serve as a proactive guide to re-invest in James Baldwin's literary work. In addition, I hope that this project will provide a new interest in the literary canon of the playwright, Howard B. Simon (along with this

Baldwin play, Simon wrote over 12 plays including the Emmy Award winning film, "Just Passin' Through").

And last, but definitely not least, it is my sincere wish to have this play revived and performed in various venues around the globe, coupled with a film adaptation for the new trans-media generation. James Baldwin once said, "You don't tell life, life tells you." And so the life journey continues.

With much gratitude, love and appreciation.

Always,

Charles Reese
Original Cast Member (James Baldwin)/ Editor/ Executive Curator, Howard B. Simon Literary Canon
Written in Paris, France
@ 18 Rue de Flandre
October 26, 2011

# WHAT PEOPLE ARE SAYING ABOUT
# JAMES BALDWIN: A SOUL ON FIRE!

*"The best sort of theatrical biography; the sort that thoroughly entertains. With humor, style and raw emotion, A Soul on Fire embraces its chosen territory with enthusiasm. All stage biographies should be served so well."*
**--David DeWitt, New York Times**

*"This play is wonderful and should be on theatre schedules around the world!"*-- **Emmy Award Winner, Doris Roberts (Everybody Loves Raymond)**

*"Playwright Howard Simon conjures up a dilemma that neatly captures the conflict Baldwin faced between his art and his activism."*
**--Charles McNulty, The Village Voice**

*" A powerful piece of theatre...everyone should experience this project!"*--**Emmy Award Nominee, CCH Pounder ( Avatar)**

*"Howard Simon's performance play, James Baldwin: A Soul on Fire is an engrossing poetic display of the religious, political, and internal turmoil that marked the life of one of the great writers of the 20th century".*--**Jeanette Toomer, Back Stage**

*The play is very moving and highly engaging. My sister, Lorraine would be honored."*--**Mamie Hansberry (sister of playwright, Lorraine Hansberry)**

*"There are only two actors in this story, but you feel the stage is filled with many more.."*--**Lisa Giordano, Show Business News**

# THE ARCHIVES

Robert Kennedy Sees Negroes About Racial Situation in North

Robert Kennedy Consults Negroes Here About North

*James Baldwin, Lorraine Hansberry and Lena Horne Are Among Those Who Warn Him of 'Explosive Situation'*

By LAYHMOND ROBINSON

Lena Horne    Lorraine Hansberry

James Baldwin

61ST ST. TUNNEL TO QUEENS SPED

*News Clippings from the actual Baldwin/Kennedy Meeting featuring Lena Horne, Lorraine Hansberry and James Baldwin circa 1963.*

*Charles Reese (James Baldwin) and Forrest McClendon (Ethereal). New Federal Theatre's Promotional Photo circa 2000. Photo Credit: Martha Holmes.*

*Baldwin Project Photo Collage: 1 & 3 - photo credit: Marsha Holmes; 2 - photo credit: Kwame Braithwaite: 4 - L-R: Sean O'Halloran (Video & Sound Design), Charles Reese, Chuck Patterson (Director), Forrest McClendon, Howard Simon (Playwright), and Laura Johnston (Stage Manager) circa 1999 at the workshop production at the Raw Space Theatre. This is the show that Woodie King Jr., witnessed and lead to the successful Off-Broadway run at the New Federal Theatre in NYC.*

*Charles Reese (James Baldwin) and Forrest Mc Clendon (Ethereal/ Peter) in James Baldwin: A Soul On Fire at the New Federal Theatre. Photo Credit: Kwame Braithwaite*

*Forrest Mc Clendon (Ethereal/ Peter) in James Baldwin: A Soul On Fire at the New Federal Theatre. Photo Credit: Kwame Braithwaite*

*Charles Reese (James Baldwin) in James Baldwin: A Soul On
Fire at the New Federal Theatre. Photo Credit:
Kwame Braithwaite*

*Performance photo from James Baldwin: A Soul on Fire circa 2000 @ New Federal Theatre. Photo credit: Kwame Braithwaite.*

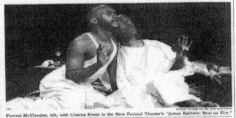

THE NEW YORK TIMES, WEDNESDAY, APRIL 13, 2000

REVIEWS

THEATER REVIEW

## Glimpsing James Baldwin on the Precipice

By DAVID DeWITT

*Cast and Crew of James Baldwin: A Soul On Fire, on set at the New Federal Theatre circa 2000. L-R: Forrest Mc Clendon, Chuck Patterson ( Director), Matt Korahais (Dramaturge),Sean O'Halloran (Video & Sound Design) and Charles Reese in the center. Photo Credit: Jacqui Casto*

*The New York Times Review on April 12, 2000 by David DeWitt. (This is the same day of the playwright, Howard B. Simon's passing).*

*Charles Reese, Forrest Mc Clendon, and David Leeming (Baldwin's Biographer) at the American Museum of Natural History in New York City during a conversation series/ screening on James Baldwin. Circa 2003*

*Howard B. Simon & Charles Reese. Morehouse College Graduation, Atlanta, GA circa 1985. This photo was taken two months before the journey to Paris, France in search of James Baldwin. Courtesy of Charles Reese.*

## HOWARD B. SIMON, PLAYWRIGHT (1962 - 2000)

Mr. Simon was born in Cleveland, OH and received his BA Degree from Morehouse College. He earned his MFA Degree from The Dramatic Writing Program at Tisch School of Arts, New York University. Mr. Simon was an educator and a member of the United Federation of the Teacher's Union. In addition to his literary canon of plays (over 12 diverse and eclectic plays); along with his collection of poetry, short stories and essays--Simon was the first recipient of the Proctor and Gamble's Dream Builder Scribe Award for his play, "Just Passin' Through." Mr. Simon also received an Emmy Award nomination for his teleplay of "Just Passin' Though." The film version also received two Emmy Awards for Best Actor and Best Production for Educational Television Programming. Mr. Simon lived in the Bedford-Stuyvesant section of Brooklyn, New York. Prior to Mr. Simon's death at the age of 37 on April 12, 2000, he was working on a new play about the poet/writer, Langston Hughes.

# THE COMPLETE LITERARY WORKS BY HOWARD B. SIMON

## FILM

JUST PASSIN. THROUGH A film written by
Howard B. Simon
(Emmy Award Winner for Best Educational
Television Programming)
Director: Jim Friedman. 1999. 60 min.

## PLAYS

JAMES BALDWIN: A SOUL ON FIRE
JUST PASSIN. THROUGH (Proctor & Gamble
Dream Builder Scribe Award Winner)
ONE OF THE CHILDREN
CALL IT CHOICE
MICA #6
UPSTAIRS APARTMENT
FREE GAY PASTEUR: THE MORALITY PLAY
SLIGHT CHANCE

PLAYS


A CONTRACT WITH AMERICA
CHANGE OF HABIT
HUSH, SOMEBODY.S CALLING MY NAME -
THE IDA B. WELLS STORY
THE RED HOUSE ON THE RED CLAY HILL-
THE BENJAMIN E. MAYS STORY
JAMES BALDWIN: A SOUL ON FIRE, PART
TWO (An Investigative Theatrical Multi-Media
Experience Bearing Witness To The Atlanta Child
Murders)

POETRY

TODAY FEELS LIKE A POEM
(Selected poetry and prose from Howard B Simon's
Purple BookSeries) Compiled and edited by Charles
Reese

For more information, please email Charles Reese,
Executive Curator of the Howard B. Simon
Literary Canon at charlesreese63@gmail.com.
www.JamesBaldwinASoulOnFire.com

**CHARLES REESE  (Editor/HB Simon Literary Canon)**

 Charles Reese is a native of Washington, D. C. who resides in Los Angeles, CA (via Brooklyn, NY) He received his Bachelor's Degree in Mass Communications/Theatre Arts from Morehouse College. He holds a certificate of completion in Theatre Performance/Management from the Burt Reynolds Theatre Institute under the tutelage of the late Master Theatre Director/Producer, Jose Quintero (in association with Florida State University). As a pro-active performing arts practitioner and cultural architect for public engagement/consultant, Charles serves as the Executor Curator for the Literary Canon of Howard B. Simon. Charles was a former student and mentee of the legendary Broadway artist, Lamar Alford (Godspell)--and also serves as the consulting curator /advisor to administer Mr. Alford's literary works. Charles is a series regular on the hit micro web comedy series, "WHO… " available only at www.ajakwetv.com. "WHO…" was an official USA selection for the first international Marseille Web Series Festival (France). Charles also serves as the official USA affiliate for The Collectif James Baldwin in Paris, France. For book signings, lectures, conversation series, speaking engagements and workshops, please contact: Penny Luedtke @ The Luedtke Agency. 212.765.9564.

Made in the USA
Charleston, SC
18 September 2012